Mariann Edgar Budde
Contempt is a Dangerous
Way to Lead a Country

ERIS
gems

JOINED BY MANY ACROSS THE COUN-
try, we have gathered this morning to pray
for unity as a nation—not for agreement,
political or otherwise, but for the kind of
unity that fosters community across diversity and division, a unity that serves the
common good.

Unity, in this sense, is the threshold re-
quirement for people to live together in
a free society, it is the solid rock, as Jesus
said, in this case upon which to build a nation. It is not conformity. It is not a victory of
one over another. It is not weary politeness
nor passivity born of exhaustion. Unity is
not partisan.

Rather, unity is a way of being with one
another that encompasses and respects differences, that teaches us to hold multiple
perspectives and life experiences as valid
and worthy of respect; that enables us, in
our communities and in the halls of power, to genuinely care for one another even
when we disagree. Those across our country
who dedicate their lives, or who volunteer,

to help others in times of natural disaster, often at great risk to themselves, never ask those they are helping for whom they voted in the past election or what positions they hold on a particular issue. We are at our best when we follow their example.

Unity at times, is sacrificial, in the way that love is sacrificial, a giving of ourselves for the sake of another. Jesus of Nazareth, in his Sermon on the Mount, exhorts us to love not only our neighbors, but to love our enemies, and to pray for those who persecute us; to be merciful, as our God is merciful, and to forgive others, as God forgives us. Jesus went out of his way to welcome those whom his society deemed as outcasts.

Now I grant you that unity, in this broad, expansive sense, is aspirational, and it's a lot to pray for—a big ask of our God, worthy of the best of who we are and can be. But there isn't much to be gained by our prayers if we act in ways that further deepen and exploit the divisions among us. Our Scriptures are quite clear that God is never impressed with prayers when actions are not informed by them. Nor does God spare us from the consequences of our deeds, which, in the end, matter more than the words we pray.

Those of us gathered here in this Cathedral are not naive about the realities of politics. When power, wealth and competing interests are at stake; when views of what America should be are in conflict; when there are strong opinions across a spectrum of possibilities and starkly different understandings of what the right course of action is, there will be winners and losers when votes are cast or decisions made that set the course of public policy and the prioritization of resources. It goes without saying that in a democracy, not everyone's particular hopes and dreams will be realized in a given legislative session or a presidential term or even a generation. Not everyone's specific prayers—for those of us who are people of prayer—will be answered as we would like. But for some, the loss of their hopes and dreams will be far more than political defeat, but instead a loss of equality, dignity, and livelihood.

Given this, is true unity among us even possible? And why should we care about it?

Well, I hope that we care, because the culture of contempt that has become normalized in our country threatens to destroy us. We are all bombarded daily with messages from what sociologists now call "the outrage industrial complex", some of it driven by external forces whose interests are furthered by a polarized America. Contempt fuels our political campaigns and social media, and many profit from it. But it's a dangerous way to lead a country.

I am a person of faith, and with God's help I believe that unity in this country is possible—not perfectly, for we are imperfect people and an imperfect union—but sufficient enough to keep us believing in and working to realize the ideals of the United States of America—ideals expressed in the Declaration of Independence, with its assertion of innate human equality and dignity.

And we are right to pray for God's help as we seek unity, for we need God's help, but only if we ourselves are willing to tend to the foundations upon which unity depends. Like Jesus' analogy of building a house of faith on the rock of his teachings, as opposed to building a house on sand, the foundations we need for unity must be sturdy enough to withstand the many storms that threaten it.

What are the foundations of unity? Drawing from our sacred traditions and texts, let me suggest that there are at least three.

The first foundation for unity is honoring the inherent dignity of every human being, which is, as all faiths represented here affirm, the birthright of all people as children of the One God. In public discourse, honoring each other's dignity means refusing to mock, discount, or demonize those with whom we differ, choosing instead to respectfully debate across our differences, and whenever possible, to seek common ground. If common ground is not possible, dignity demands that we remain true to our convictions without contempt for those who hold convictions of their own.

A second foundation for unity is honesty in both private conversation and public discourse. If we aren't willing to be honest, there is no use in praying for unity, because our actions work against the prayers themselves. We might, for a time, experience a false sense of unity among some, but not the sturdier, broader unity that we need to address the challenges we face.

Now to be fair, we don't always know where the truth lies, and there is a lot working against the truth now, staggeringly so. But when we do know what is true, it's incumbent upon us to speak the truth, even when—and especially when—it costs us.

A third foundation for unity is humility, which we all need, because we are all fallible human beings. We make mistakes. We say and do things that we regret. We have our blind spots and biases, and we are perhaps the most dangerous to ourselves and others when we are persuaded, without a doubt, that we are absolutely right and someone else is absolutely wrong. Because then we are just a few steps away from labeling ourselves as the good people, versus the bad people.

The truth is that we are all people, capable of both good and bad. Aleksandr Solzhenitsyn astutely observed that "The line separating good and evil passes not through states, nor between classes, nor between political parties, but right through every human heart and through all human hearts." The more we realize this, the more room we have within ourselves for humility, and openness to one another across our differences, because in fact, we are more like one another than we realize, and we need each other.

Unity is relatively easy to pray for on occasions of solemnity. It's a lot harder to realize when we're dealing with real differences in the public arena. But without unity, we are building our nation's house on sand.

With a commitment to unity that incorporates diversity and transcends disagreement, and the solid foundations of dignity, honesty, and humility that such unity requires, we can do our part, in our time, to help realize the ideals and the dream of America.

Let me make one final plea, Mr President. Millions have put their trust in you. As you told the nation yesterday, you have felt the providential hand of a loving God. In the name of our God, I ask you to have mercy upon the people in our country who are scared now. There are gay, lesbian and transgender children in Democratic, Republican and independent families who fear for their lives.

And the people who pick our crops and clean our office buildings; who labor in our poultry farms and meat-packing plants; who wash the dishes after we eat in restaurants and work the night shift in hospitals—they may not be citizens or have the proper documentation, but the vast majority of immigrants are not criminals. They pay taxes, and are good neighbors. They are faithful members of our churches, mosques and synagogues, gurdwara, and temples.

Have mercy, Mr President, on those in our communities whose children fear that their parents will be taken away. Help those who are fleeing war zones and persecution in their own lands to find compassion and welcome here. Our God teaches us that we are to be merciful to the stranger, for we were once strangers in this land.

May God grant us all the strength and courage to honor the dignity of every human being, speak the truth in love, and walk humbly with one another and our God, for the good of all the people of this nation and the world.

ERIS

265 Riverside Dr.
New York, NY 10025

This is a textual reproduction of the sermon
delivered on January 21, 2025, by the Bishop of
Washington in the presence of the newly inaugu-
rated President Trump.

ISBN 978-1-916809-40-6

eris.press